Secrets of my Prison House

Geoffrey Gatza

Secrets of my Prison House

Geoffrey Gatza

BlazeVOX [books]

Buffalo, New York

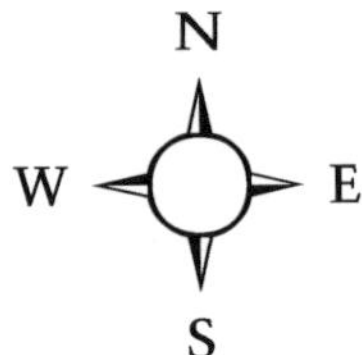
N
W   E
S

B   X

Acknowledgments

With great thanks to Bill Berkson, Tom Clark, Hoa Nguyen, Michael Kelleher, Lori Desormeaux, Just Buffalo Literary Center, the New Philadelphia Poets, CD Wright, Donna White, the man dressed as a clown who was lost in NYC and allowed me to take his picture. And to you, yes you, the one reading this bit, thank you for picking up this book, hurray:-)

Also, great thanks the editors and publishers of these projects some of these poems have appeared. Hurray on you!

+ Poet-Editors Feature at Otolith

+ Anthology: 50/50: Words & Images for Didi Menendez; editors Grace Cavalieri, and April Carter Grant

+ Hauntology of Smoke and Ochre: an anthology inspired by the life and death of Ingrid Jonker;. South Africa

+ A/SH Anthology: Fact-Simile

+ Poets for Living Waters — a poetry action in response to the BP Gulf oil disaster

Table of Contents

Secrets of my Prison House

The Sandra Bullock Story that Stunned us All

At the height of all this
The fears turned to joy

Maybe in another lifetime
We can have beads on our birthday

I may be old but I am not dead
I am staying alive
In the golden crayon of choice

As simple as designing new waste
I hear babies cry

You can safely say
The crowd goes wild

Get your tickets today

Everybody Has An Ashbery Of Their Own

There are no recommendations
I cannot tell you how butter tastes
I could barely stand up; there was a car crash

Everything starts with potting soil
Until I found a wafer that goes beyond

When you grow up
Find out which transitions are right for you
Find out which nutrients are best

We do not know.
A poem cannot prove
That cornbread crumbs won the Kentucky Derby

Spoken from the heart, the levies broke
The idea runs counter to the team effort

For the first time I can tell you of the poison plot
Giving me more time to do the things I love

Sometimes you need tomorrow to recover from today
Some enjoy telling the adventure more than experiencing

A slow drive with a friend, stopping to go
suffering a disaster, but the small talk is all tennis courts

I am far from my homeland.
The building is in ruins; the hurt and loss is adoption
Of a new language of deficit with few creature comforts

With a helping hand and open broadcast,
I hope to see you tomorrow evening, right here.

Will She Return to Dancing with the Stars

To make it official
I do not think of myself as a home wrecker

The cover that is making headlines
is of me wearing a bunny suit

I have this little baby with me
The house is under construction

Writing a check is easy
I choked up during my speech
I know I will always be welcome here

I was able to give
And kickass somewhere!
What a wonderful world

We had been matched
I thought it was important

We went through all the steps
I want to thank all the moms

Making sure no one knew
we had been married for a year

Taking this day-by-day
before the vultures descend

His mistakes are mistakes he himself must address
The love of my adopted hometown restored my faith

This is how I looked in the security camera
The bouncer let her in for free
I think this was revenge for my awesome hair

The Conk-Singleton Forgery Case

and I have myself found it a very soothing atmosphere

but you have a kinder heart over these long years.
I fill my glass with whiskey and ice and the oily pleasure
with which he does his evil. To deal with the case

and the dog that was the Sussex Vampire's first victim.
Then there was the mongoose swelling into small lakes on either side.
Our guide paused at the mouth of this bridge

With hope. Our hope is an Easter hope:
that in the face of death and deterioration
and picking up his hat he turned to the door

alone

almost like visiting a chapel. It is how history unfolds onto paper
and how one can display one bit that unfolds layer of relevant history
upon personal interest that makes the curator an artist!

Tempus Fidget

Poetry expects poets to do their duty
Ex nihlo nihlo fit

The leaves are attacking
we get terribly excited

butter grows in blocks on butter branches

ninety-nine out of one hundred times we get let down
concentrating extraordinarily hard on a miniature desk

It was a hundred quid human drawing
A series of washes in varied gray
A young constable on a bridge with rope

There is only the color of the paper beneath our words
Right to the skies, the clouds adequately describe water
The intense way artists tend to render fatback
It's most interesting and translates into money

A generation later
our investments are not good

My grand-daughter is sick and tired of losing
Her antique writings to something like this

Now is the time
a rainbow sheen
to move your trust.

All that is lacking is audacity and opportunity,
wealth to be poured into a very plain silver cup.

Fantasia Lights, Too
For Kristianne, Ted and Mark

It's the smell of a wolf or a Hello Kitty with a strap-on, one can't help but think how cute, how responsibility and desire are conflicting elements, how that dildo is going to put someone's eye out; sometimes art hurts. You smell astroglide and look at three cats and a man telling you how he ran from Bigfoot when he was fourteen, then on to discussing how a spice weasel is a fact not an interpretation, you don't need a rocket surgeon to tell you that. A philosophical problem is not an empirical problem. You drive past the restaurant you should be having dinner at with someone you have wanted to shake by the hand for years now. He drives fast and talks in scarce thoughts of exaggerated passions, subjects from the army to anger and how no one gets caught growing, he knew a guy. The endless social questions of what a poem is and how the fuck can anyone write a poem and that be grounds for an art form. Steel is heavy, steel is art. He hit the dashboard and then asked if I liked Neil Diamond. I said I heard he can split a room, he asked who I heard that from, I told him, Boswell and he nodded like he knew him, recognized the disdain some hold against him for saying that thing; but no I know he doesn't know him or anything more on this, but that was how this truck ride tapped along, blindly regaining its footing. It's been ten days without marijuana and one gets jangly, uncomfortably so, so discomforted you call friends, all your friends whom you have ever put bowl to mouth with, just in case they do not actually know of anyone who they can call for a quick favor. You call your dealer to let him know that there is a poetry book fair going on just in case he may not know, and I know he would have called if he had heard from his regular supplier, but this is to let him know the cultural aspects of the city. We will suppose that this is not about that but this, and say off hand how this affects the other, it's a zinger coming down from the sunny haze where a patron can potentially knock knees with someone who you had a twitter fight with yesterday, and you cannot gather up the courage to apologize just yet; the stomach flips on emptiness'. Then a call comes in from the ex-wife of an exlife and that strained excitement begins to surge through your memories, everything works out and in minutes you'll be dining on rogan josh, high as a kite and pretend that all is fine and a smooth transition back to normal is a dinner jacket rented to you by the maître d'hôtel. You dream of impressing the person who has impressed you for so many years, you hope he doesn't smell the pot smell, or if he does will want to smoke some with you. But now, we are parked across the street of that restaurant and that dinner in a patch of lawn that is not a parking space an hour past the time agreed to meet. The dealer is not at home and he comes back to the truck to call on his cell phone. We drive up Elmwood to her house in hopes she might be there. He tells me of his time in the Army and how he blackmailed his sergeant major with the names and locations of his hookers, I really liked him at this point. But I would like him better if he had the pot and we were talking crazy shit while high. So it was me waiting in the truck again, crinkling a smiling towards a church going grandmother walking towards her car from the nearby liquor store. I could tell she thought I was a cop. I wanted to get away from all of this but if it all worked out; well, then fine. But if I had come this close to only smell the declining disappointment of a faded world; well we never had to figure that out because out he came and in your face, he had two ounces of commercial and a small bit of some really tasty kind bud. We smoked a bit of the kind and I let him keep the rest as a thank you for the troubles. He yammered on and on as he drove around the place I had to get out, a poetry reading in Allentown. But the more I smoked the easier the stories were to digest. He told me of guns and tattoos and of a giant rat that I am certain the world is not yet ready to hear. But I will tell you of the worst smell I have encountered outside of a war zone and preteen narco-fascist artists; a poet who made another artist gasp and demand an explanation; a brief encounter of Akron love, The only authentic man in the room is not sure if he is a fraud, of the man who led the way out of blue death with two gay cats Marcel and Balthazar under his arms, of the kindness and thoughtful friends who you can fight with and come to hug over art, of the UPS truck that sent books from South Carolina to Kenmore in nine hours, and how four pearls made me fall down stairs and dislocate my elbow. But that last one is not as interesting a story as once I put the pearls back in their container, instantly I regain my fortune, my land and title are restored, and like a guillotine everything falls into place. I get that phone call that began this garish affair. To sum up, there is very good evidence that we generally don't truly want good poetry; but rather poetry that confirms our assumptions. We may believe in the clash of opinions; instead we embed ourselves in the reassuring tomb of an echo. Dangerous fun at a youthful twenty-five makes for a queasy freefall at a gray haired forty.

20 Things I Need To Tell You

for Didi Menendez

1. You have that Cary Grant elegance

2. He shot her right in the baby

3. What you cannot cure, you must endure

4. Well, strike me up a gum tree

5. He is mercurial in nature

6. That comes from reading books without pictures

7. The game is not worth the candle

8. Pick the bones out of that one

9. He sails very close to the wind

10. Put a different spin on the family sitcom

11. Television is that great friendly soul

12. It was like going to work in a mine, only fun

13. John made sure to retain a part of his life

14. The more people I meet, the more I like cats

15. Poetry no longer exists

16. Physics cannot prove it anymore

17. Sure enough, I did get a lot of money

18. You feel safe and secure when I am there

19. Forget the billing, this one is on the house

20. I cannot thank you enough, I love you and all that you have brought
    into my life and when you travel onwards, please take a small sprig of
    rosemary and tuck it in a sachet with ramps, thyme and lavender to
    remember me by

St. John of God
Patron saint of booksellers
Goes to AWP

For Bernie Rhodenbarr

The animal shall not be measured by man. In a world older and more complete than ours, they move finished and complete, gifted with extension of the senses we have lost or never attained, living by voices we shall never hear. They are not brethren; they are not underlings; they are other nations, caught with ourselves in the net of life and time, fellow prisoners of the splendor and travail of the earth.

—Henry Beston, naturalist and author (1888-1968)

o   He was all Dr. Jekyll / Paulie Shore

Conjure up the classic image of a humanities or social sciences professor, the fields where the imbalance is greatest: tweed jacket, pipe, nerdy, longwinded, secular and liberal. Even though that may be an outdated stereotype, it influences younger people's ideas about what they want to be when they grow up.

o   Winterception

he's been an absolute tiger
Thick as thieves they
quest to tame the restive region

o   The democracy manqué

self-harm
meticulous
the art form that shapes the world
exuberance

o   Cannibal cookies

Not too distant horizon
What do you want? I wanted so many things I couldn't respond
Let me have a look at you.
Look noble and refined
Those that look bereft and in need, seldom receive it

o   Cinnamon Acetaminophen

He has proved to be a broken reed

o   I'm too lazy to be a transvestite

A thing in nature without a flaw is in itself a flaw. Beauty is in the eye of the beholder; and I behold something beautiful, my boy.

o   A true friend fact checks

embrace of midnight debauchery
sheer malarkey
raucous
escapements
dour and repressed

o   Preposterous Prepositions

Great ideas take time, effort, and perseverance. There are countless dead ends and failures along the way

o   Ray Federman is no Dominic Dunne

but also to live, as patisseries do, absorbed in the repetitive, ritualized, and
seemingly timeless practices of their art.

monkish or self-sacrificing

o   I don't know what you do with your head

dignified moderation and temporal respect
forget the travails and bad

she could no longer countenance being a member
in that multi-modal and multilayered bungalow

plummeted

o   Thought Violence

I'd rather speak to the cat

Perspicacity — synonyms: acumen, sagacity, discernment, shrewdness,
insight, penetration, acuteness, and clairvoyance. Someone who is
perspicacious notices, realizes, and understands things quickly.

It was all piffle
imbroglio
implacable / implacably
often thought of as difficult, remote and unattractive

o   Fourive / Fourevif

to a considerable extent or degree.
completely, wholly, or entirely.
actually, really, or truly.

Kill two birds with one cat

o   I, egg, lightly beaten

He is so old school it's almost endearing. He's been making poetry for
nearly 40 years and continues to make them just as he pleases, even if that
means he's completely out of step with a younger, more unruly generation.

Stopoped

~

In the same way the peacock's tail evolved into a flamboyantly useless appendage, words have had to resort to ludicrous contortions to stand out. Inspired by the movement of candlelight, Stopoped is an amalgam of words, supposedly from the "ignore them, they're just trying to get attention" school of poetry. So far we're just not sure if this is a comedy, a tragedy or some surreal, hallucinogenic fairy tale, neverumind

just eat them.

Stopoped

Buffailo

Hopefulalo

Wonothingder

Donutkite

entrianglement

Dandelightion

Dogrowthouse

Sidecidewalk

Languacamolege

Velociphilatelist

Windsocknuckle

baseraseball

mirroustaboutr

squirrevolve

Frolicmimic

Capitalizsinge

blockadvisehead

fashionpapergirl

wargriefgel

hamburgerwaffle

disappflyointment

conservativeforpay

daiseychainrecluse

antiquenettles

hornswinceoggle

prizemittenscout

fountaintedhead

mildewfigmeadow

moderndutchcowcreamer

applebowlerhead

solicitwitter

disturbaneing

conjecturetinctures

hoggishkipperslumber

imbibeakerintuition

buzzfoxsaddlehound

purplelobsterfiend

pageboymyfoot

gingershwindows

nonchalantprovocation

pleasantpheasant

mottledoystereyes

mujuiciestang

agreenlulutown

precipitatedpotato

torturethemnotus

howbadisamerica

laughghanistan

tomorningrow

priparableson

messengermination

racconcannon

giraffederation

unsultimatelystainable

fabulinequitablyzed

allegoriesetraps

winsomevision

bandadventurege

scotchopen

Gutenbergobsolete

fashionlightenment

quillorderideal

fripepperies

communworthy

depreconveyate

challengiantshoes

owncommentaudiences

shiftingoundorlds

bookayakblock

graceworpple

confessoroofig

onomatomania

onomatomania

Noun:

An obsession with particular words or names and desire to recall or repeat them.

Etymology:

Via Latin, from Greek onoma (name) + -mania (excessive enthusiasm or craze).

Thankverymuchyou

Incorrigiblefuckbungler

OnshotChristmasdeadeve

Lordloveaduck

Fatherreunitedson

Total beef recall

Explosiveignitiondevice

Bittermurderalmonds

Don'tbeabsurd

Stunnedseemedsurprised

Waterhappeningboarding

Davenportsportscontest

Goodunitedstatesevil

Baseballfoot

Yellowgarbagemanvest

Snowchristmasrain

So*fly*up

Somethingalzheimersanything

cautionatmospherequestion

Threatarttreat

Whatdotimewebegin

Burdentobelieve

Brutalcriminalintelligence

Lookbacktogoforward

end

I am Forbid To Tell
the Secrets of my Prison House

I was feeling a bit out of sorts after leaving my group of friends behind in a local bar after a brief altercation with a very rude waitress. They decided to stay at the bar, I assume because they had settled in and the offence was not directed towards them. So I was on the street walking in a light misty rain. With a certain sense of gallantry I was going to find my own way.

1. Mollified

He was polite and very kind, a kindness that was rather dull. A silent sort of dullness one enjoys while reading the morning newspaper with a dear friend. His eyes were gray and empty giving his face a blank understanding that said he had seen everything eyes can see. Steady eyes that would not be surprised by anything said or done. I thought he simply had a sleepless night, likely a nap would do him good. He had an easy-going temperament that summed him up by saying he never had one real thought and kept no deep philosophies. A sensible maturity that could be relied on through hard times; he could, as they say, steer an even keel.

2. Taciturn

He seldom went out anymore preferring to hold dinner parties in his
home. Enjoying the company of friends gathered close by but far
away from the rest of the world.

It took several moments for astonishment to show itself on his face.
When speech returned to him he said, Propinquity brings these things
out.

3. Dyspeptic

He spent the better part of his life wanting to go to New York, and I
was very over the hubbub of that city. I wanted to see this city and all
it's charm. He too was over his city and could no longer see the
beauty it beheld. We didn't understand each other really. But we both
knew that we each had that odd golden desire to want more than what
was around them.

4. Prominent

Yes my friend, I worry about you Americans. Your need to be entertained all day long is a worrying thing. You forget what silence sounds like. It sounds like this. We stopped and listened to the forest rumble along. It is never silent for very long, but if you listen for it, it will find you.

The elephant on their shoulders just got heavier.

5. Charming

Beyond our ken

But you did these things, I said. Yes I did them, she said carefully. I did them only because of your presence; your nearness brought this out of me.

There was something very sly and secretive about him.

I have made enough money in my life to satisfy my wants and caprices.
Of all soups made or eaten, I have to say that this is the best pea soup I have ever eaten.

6. Held his breath

I think you are going cheerfully to your death.

I told him we could be friends but I delicately intoned that I would never
be able to acknowledge him in public.

My wife and I, as the vulgar would say, had words.
To be accurate it was eighty-seven words to her and five for me.

7. Hear a pin drop

Thirty-eight years old and in the prime of life. Slim and vigorous, with
a very upright posture. Those clear blue eyes, which looked so hard at
the immediate view that they seemed to see right past it toward some
distant horizon. A serious brow, and firmly pressed lips, expressive of
his steadfastness. You might not pick him out of a crowd unless you
heard his voice - vibrant, with rich harmonics, making everything he
said almost more impressive than it was, you might think, with its
resonance, its rhythmic sense and its clear intonations, except that
through it came the deep conviction behind his words

He was good-looking in a stern sort of way, with a strong chin, a
determined mouth and an intent and penetrating gaze. While his
manner was often reserved or gruff, his intimidating exterior
concealed a man of passion, kindness and humor.

8. In perplexity

I'm talking to the engineer not the oil rag, he said to my companion
with a scornful look. Then in a quick wipe of his face, turned to me
with a warm smile and said,

Some people enjoy telling their adventures more than experiencing
them.

9. Inquisitively

An unattractive woman said, well I asked Henry and he agreed. I
assumed that Henry was quite an affable soul who probably out of
personal safety always found it best to agree with her.

I told her I was in town for a funeral.

Oh, you remember, she said. He did not remember at all, but politely
assisted the situation.

Sometimes death is not tragic.

10.   Authoritatively

When the two boys returned to the table, their plates were filled with desserts. Only desserts sat on their plates and no actual dinner. It was very funny to see. One boy's mother politely scolded him that there was no meat or vegetables on his plate. But this is for after your dinner she said. Slyly he said that this was merely kid's stuff. His friend readily agreed by nodding his head slowly chewing on a cookie. There was a form of logic in his answer that could not, with good grace, be argued with.

What a lovely place I said to her. She looked at me oddly and said, really, I always thought it a bit plain. I said, what a wonderful luxury.

Put a pin in that balloon.

Delightful Fugue

adorable remembrance

a-ok sores

absorbing precious pasts

acceptable with baser matter

adequate by heaven

admirable woman

admissible smiling tables

agreeable uncle

all right adieu remember me

alluring come please come

ambrosial wonderful

amiable must think it

amusing villain

angelic knave

appealing right

appropriate we shake hands

at rest as it is

attractive whirling words

average honest ghost

beauteous scholars

beautiful request

best in mind

bewitching in faith

big swear on my sword

boffo

camp gentlemen

campy swear

captivating of day and night

cared for and dreamt of

champion antique disposition

charismatic encountered thus

charming know aught of me

cheerful deed

cheeringly swear

cheery spirit

choice on the floor

classy gentlemen

clever with fingers on lips

comely I pray

comical time

common spite

complacent to set it right

congenial night

contented notes

convenient marvelously wise

cooking with gas, very well said

cool dancers

copacetic encompassment

cozy distant knowledge

crack to mark

cut up know not well

cute very wild

cute addicted

dainty dishonor

dandy take heed

darling fencing

dazzling quarrel

dear faith

decent charge

delectable faith of wit

delicate working

delicious crimes

delightful does he this?

deluxe questions

desirable merry

dishy I know the gentleman

diverting as such

divine tennis

dreamy house of sale

droll observations

easy matter

electrifying affrighted

elegant doublet

enamoring fouled

Geoffrey Gatza is the editor and Publisher of BlazeVOX [books] and the author of eight books of poetry; Secrets of my Prison House is his most recent. Kenmore: Poem Unlimited and Not So Fast Robespierre are now available from Menendez Publishing. HouseCat Kung Fu: Strange Poems for Wild Children is also available from Meritage Press. He lives in Buffalo, NY with his girlfriend and two cats.

http://www.geoffreygatza.com/
http://www.blazevox.org

Made in the USA
Charleston, SC
22 July 2010